ideal

ID3405

D0478253

Fraction Dice Games

Patricia Cartland Noble

Published by Ideal School Supply
An imprint of McGraw-Hill Children's Publishing
Copyright © 2000 McGraw-Hill Children's Publishing

Art Director: Sara Mordecai
Cover Designer: Theresa Tomlin
Production Designer: Piper Brown
Illustrator: Duane Bibby
Editor: Ann Roper
Project Editor: Jill Osofsky
Project Coordinator: Judy Crum

Send all inquiries to:
McGraw-Hill Children's Publishing
3195 Wilson Drive NW
Grand Rapids, MI 49544

All Rights Reserved • Printed in the United States of America.

Fraction Dice Games–Grades 3–6
ISBN: 1-56451-327-0

**McGraw-Hill
Children's Publishing**

CONTENTS

∎∎

Teacher's Notes	3
Game 1: Fraction Five-In-A-Row	5
Game 2: Divvy it Up!	7
Game 3: How Does Your Garden Grow?	9
Game 4: Six Pies for Sale!	11
Game 5: Whole Numbers in Hiding	13
Game 6: Less Than, Equal To, or Greater Than One?	15
Game 7: The 10K Challenge	17
Game 8: Measuring Magic Beans	19
Game 9: One Dozen Doughnuts	21
Game 10: Equivalent Fraction Four-Square	23
Game 11: Equivalent Fraction Tic-Tac-Toe	25
Game 12: Sum It Summit	27
Game 13: High or Low?	29
Game 14: Sum-Difference	31

TEACHER'S NOTES

Fraction Dice Games is full of fun and learning for students! Fraction concepts can be particularly challenging for students in the upper elementary grades. This collection of 14 games will provide ample practice for skill review, maintenance, and retention during a unit of study and throughout the year. The games are designed to strengthen students' understanding of fractions as described in current mathematics standards.

The games include a wide range of skills that are sequenced by level of difficulty. Games 1 – 3 involve a basic understanding of fractions—how they are represented and the meaning of *numerator* and *denominator*. In Game 2, for example, students are given an opportunity to divide regions into equal parts. This skill is surprisingly challenging for many students, since many worksheets do this for them. In the next three games students work with fractions greater than one, as in Game 4, *Six Pies for Sale!*, that requires students to record fractions and mixed numbers simultaneously. In Game 7, *The 10K Challenge*, students record distances as both common fractions and decimal fractions. In the next game students practice the real-life skill of measuring, in this case, magic beans. Game 9 offers practice in identifying fractional parts of a set. Students practice recognizing equivalent fractions as they play familiar games such as Four-Square and Tic-Tac-Toe. The last three games involve adding fractions having like and unlike denominators. In the final game, students also subtract fractions.

The dice game format is inviting to students, making skill practice an exciting experience. The skills used in these games are highlighted at the top of each page and directions are organized in an easy-to-follow sequence:

Ready tells how many people, what dice to use, and the materials needed.

Set tells how to set up the game for play.

Play gives rules, procedures, and tells how the winner is determined.

Play Again describes a variation of the game to provide additional, and often more challenging, practice.

Two fraction dice labeled $\frac{1}{2}$, $\frac{1}{3}$, $\frac{1}{4}$, $\frac{1}{6}$, $\frac{1}{8}$, $\frac{1}{12}$ and $\frac{1}{2}$, $\frac{2}{3}$, $\frac{3}{4}$, $\frac{5}{6}$, $\frac{7}{8}$, $\frac{11}{12}$, plus one regular die labeled 1, 2, 3, 4, 5, 6 are required for the games. Stickers are provided in the book so you or the students can make the fraction dice required to play the games. Note that Fraction Dice and Blank Dice are available from Ideal School Supply. Please see a current Ideal School Supply catalog, contact your local educational dealer, or visit the web site at **www.idealschoolsupply.com**.

Games can be introduced as a whole-class activity. Play a few rounds with the students to build their interest and clarify the game rules. Make a transparency of the game board and play on the overhead projector. Use this as an opportunity to review and discuss fraction ideas within the context of a game.

As students play these games, they will work with a variety of fraction models including regions, sets, and fractions on a number line, in order to develop a broad understanding of their many representations. They may play the games in pairs or in groups, thus encouraging mathematical discussion. Many of the game boards can be used to assess students' progress. In addition, valuable information can be gained through observing and questioning students as they practice skills in each game. Ask questions such as: *What does this mean? How do you know? What will you do next? Why? Is there another way to name the fraction?* to assess their understanding. Many games can be adjusted to students' skill levels by changing the dice or modifying the game board. The **Play Again** suggestion for each game gives ideas for such adjustments or modifications.

Enjoy the games!

FRACTION FIVE-IN-A-ROW

Skills

Understand the meaning of fractions: as parts of a whole, as parts of a collection, and as a point on a number line

Know the meaning of numerator and denominator

Ready

Small group

Regular die labeled 1 to 6

Pencils

Game board for each player

Set

Roll the die to see who begins. The player who rolls a 3, or the number closest to 3, begins. Play proceeds in a clockwise direction.

Play

Take turns rolling the die. Use the number rolled to write either the numerator or the denominator of one of the fractions shown on the game board. The numerator is the **shaded** part of each region or set, or the dot on the number line. Check each other's thinking.

If you cannot use a number rolled, your turn ends.

The player who correctly writes five fractions in a row in any direction is the winner.

Play Again

Include equivalent fractions to name pictures.

FRACTION FIVE-IN-A-ROW

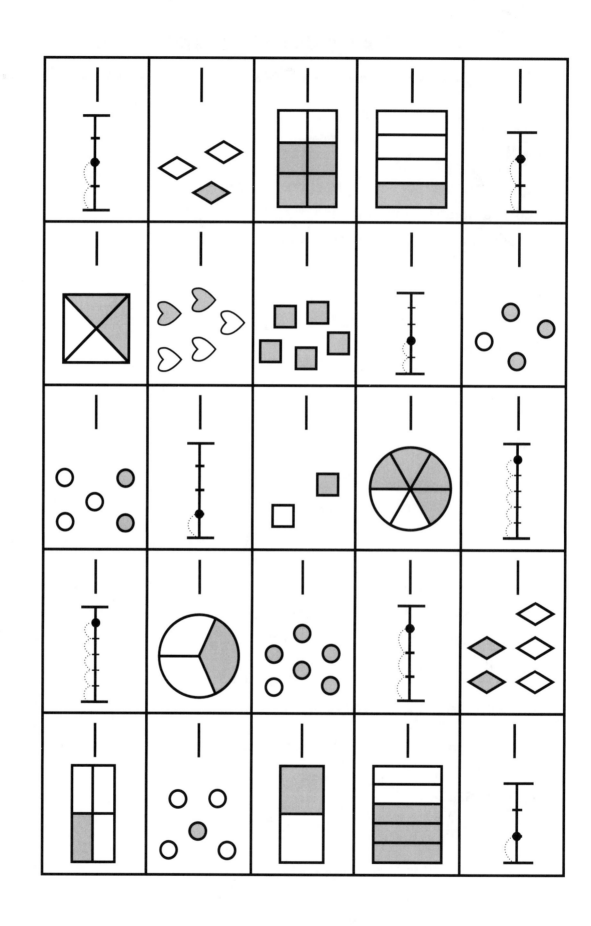

Skills

Divide a region into equal parts

Compare simple fractions

Develop understanding of fractions as parts of a unit whole

Know the meaning of *numerator* and *denominator*

Ready

Two players

Make a fraction die labeled $\frac{1}{2}$, $\frac{1}{3}$, $\frac{2}{3}$, $\frac{1}{4}$, $\frac{2}{4}$, $\frac{3}{4}$

Pencils

One game board

Set

The player who has the shorter first name begins.

Play

Roll the die and write that fraction in the box for Round 1. Divide and shade the region to show the fraction. Compare the two fractions. Circle the smaller fraction. If two fractions show the same amount ($\frac{1}{2}$ and $\frac{2}{4}$), you may both circle your fraction. Continue for five rounds.

The player who has circled more fractions is the winner.

Play Again

Circle the larger fraction.

And Again!

Make a different die. Label it with six of these fractions: $\frac{1}{8}$, $\frac{1}{3}$, $\frac{1}{4}$, $\frac{1}{2}$, $\frac{2}{8}$, $\frac{2}{3}$, $\frac{3}{8}$, $\frac{3}{4}$, $\frac{6}{8}$

DIVVY IT UP!

Player 1:   Player 2:

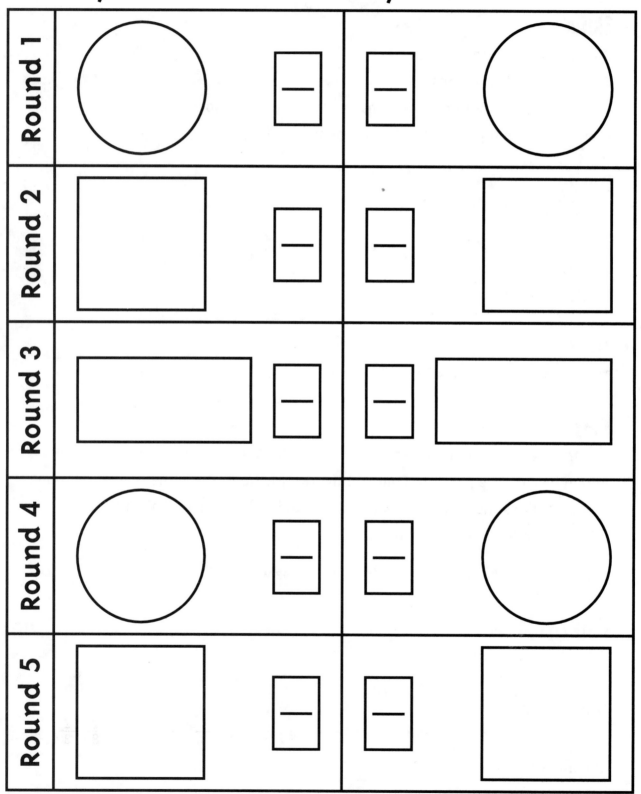

HOW DOES YOUR GARDEN GROW?

Skills

Understand fractions as parts of a whole
Know the meaning of *numerator* and *denominator*

Ready

Small group
Two fraction dice labeled $\frac{1}{2}$, $\frac{1}{3}$, $\frac{1}{4}$, $\frac{1}{6}$, $\frac{1}{8}$, $\frac{1}{12}$ and $\frac{1}{2}$, $\frac{2}{3}$, $\frac{3}{4}$, $\frac{5}{6}$, $\frac{7}{8}$, $\frac{11}{12}$
Favorite color crayons
Game board for each player

Set

The player whose name is first alphabetically begins. Play proceeds in a clockwise direction.

Play

Take turns rolling the dice. Color flower parts to show the fractions you roll. Continue until someone completes both flowers.

If you cannot use a fraction, your turn ends. You may also choose to skip a turn. This may happen if you need $\frac{11}{12}$. Rather than hoping to roll $\frac{1}{12}$ eleven times, you may choose to hold out for one roll of $\frac{11}{12}$.

You may not divide fractions between flowers, or use parts of fractions. For example, if there is $\frac{1}{4}$ remaining on one flower part and you roll $\frac{3}{4}$, your turn ends because you cannot use the entire fraction.

The player who is first to color both flowers is the winner.

Play Again

For two players. Use the die labeled $\frac{1}{2}$, $\frac{1}{3}$, $\frac{1}{4}$, $\frac{1}{6}$, $\frac{1}{8}$, $\frac{1}{12}$. Use two different colors and one game board. The players may color both flowers. The player who colors the last part to complete the flowers is the winner.

HOW DOES YOUR GARDEN GROW?

...By halves, thirds, fourths, sixths, eighths, and twelfths!

Skills

Count by fractional parts to show whole units from 1 to 6

Model and write fractions greater than 1 as mixed numbers, whole numbers, and improper fractions

Add fractions having like denominators

Ready

Small group

Make a fraction die labeled $\frac{1}{8}$, $\frac{2}{8}$, $\frac{3}{8}$, $\frac{4}{8}$, $\frac{5}{8}$, $\frac{6}{8}$

Crayons or colored markers

Game board for each player

Set

The player who has the longest hair begins. Play proceeds in a clockwise direction.

Play

Roll the die. The fraction you roll shows how many **eighths** of a pie you buy. Color that fraction of one pie. Record the fraction you roll. Record the running total as a fraction and as a mixed number. Continue playing in the same way. Each time the die is rolled, color the pie, and record the running total as a fraction and a mixed number.

If you roll a fraction you cannot use, your turn ends. The first player to color exactly six pies is the winner.

Play Again

Make a game board having pies divided into fourths or sixths. Make a fraction die labeled $\frac{1}{4}$, $\frac{2}{4}$, $\frac{3}{4}$, $\frac{4}{4}$, $\frac{5}{4}$, $\frac{6}{4}$ or $\frac{1}{6}$, $\frac{2}{6}$, $\frac{3}{6}$, $\frac{4}{6}$, $\frac{5}{6}$, $\frac{6}{6}$. Add by fourths or sixths to make whole pies.

SIX PIES FOR SALE!

You know the rhyme, "Simple Simon met a pie man..." In this game, you are the pie man and you have six whole pies to sell at the fair. Roll the die to see how many **eighths** you sell at a time.

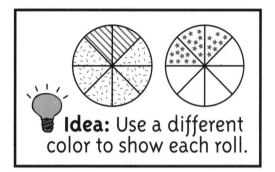

Idea: Use a different color to show each roll.

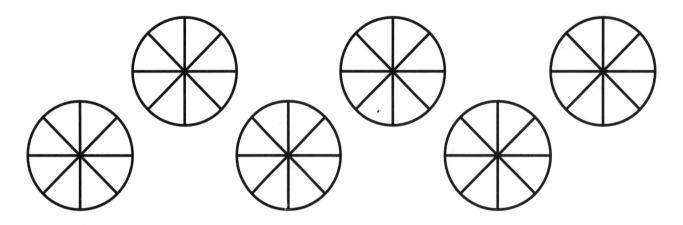

After each roll, record the total amount of pie you have sold. Write each amount in two ways.

Roll	Fraction rolled	Total eighths	Mixed or whole number	Roll	Fraction rolled	Total eighths	Mixed or whole number
1				7			
2				8			
3				9			
4				10			
5				11			
6				12			

WHOLE NUMBERS IN HIDING

Skill

Recognize whole numbers as fractions

Ready

Small group

Regular die labeled 1 to 6

Color markers or crayons

Game board for each player

Set

The player who has the shortest last name begins. Play proceeds in a clockwise direction. Each player uses a different color marker or crayon.

Play

Roll the die. Color the space on the board that names the whole number you roll as a fraction. Example: You roll a 4. You may color the fraction $\frac{12}{3}$.

The first player to color a path from the top of the board to the bottom (Start to Finish) is the winner. The spaces in the path must connect by sides, not corners.

Play Again

For two players. Use one game board and two different color markers or crayons. The spaces in the path may touch sides and corners.

WHOLE NUMBERS IN HIDING

Start							
$\frac{3}{3}$	$\frac{12}{2}$	$\frac{12}{3}$	$\frac{24}{6}$	$\frac{9}{3}$	$\frac{15}{3}$	$\frac{5}{5}$	$\frac{24}{4}$
$\frac{18}{3}$	$\frac{4}{2}$	$\frac{4}{4}$	$\frac{12}{2}$	$\frac{8}{8}$	$\frac{8}{2}$	$\frac{5}{1}$	$\frac{20}{4}$
$\frac{10}{2}$	$\frac{60}{10}$	$\frac{4}{4}$	$\frac{20}{10}$	$\frac{16}{4}$	$\frac{24}{8}$	$\frac{8}{4}$	$\frac{10}{10}$
$\frac{24}{4}$	$\frac{10}{5}$	$\frac{8}{2}$	$\frac{12}{4}$	$\frac{18}{3}$	$\frac{1}{1}$	$\frac{10}{2}$	$\frac{25}{5}$
$\frac{15}{5}$	$\frac{20}{4}$	$\frac{6}{6}$	$\frac{25}{5}$	$\frac{6}{3}$	$\frac{20}{4}$	$\frac{9}{3}$	$\frac{10}{2}$
$\frac{25}{5}$	$\frac{8}{8}$	$\frac{15}{3}$	$\frac{6}{1}$	$\frac{2}{2}$	$\frac{15}{3}$	$\frac{10}{10}$	$\frac{12}{2}$
$\frac{30}{10}$	$\frac{18}{3}$	$\frac{50}{10}$	$\frac{16}{4}$	$\frac{24}{6}$	$\frac{12}{2}$	$\frac{12}{6}$	$\frac{40}{10}$
Finish							

Skill

Recognize and write fractions that are less than, equal to, and greater than one

Ready

Two players

Regular die labeled 1 to 6

Pencils

One game board

Set

The player who rolls the higher number goes first.

Play

Take turns rolling the die. Write the number you roll as a numerator or denominator to make a fraction that belongs in one of the groups:

<1 (less than one), $=1$ (equal to one), or >1 (greater than one).

Check each other's fractions.

If you cannot use a number you roll, your turn ends.

The first player to complete nine fractions correctly is the winner.

Play Again

Add part of one more fraction to each box and play again in the same way.

LESS THAN, EQUAL TO, OR GREATER THAN ONE?

Player 1: _____   **Player 2:** _____

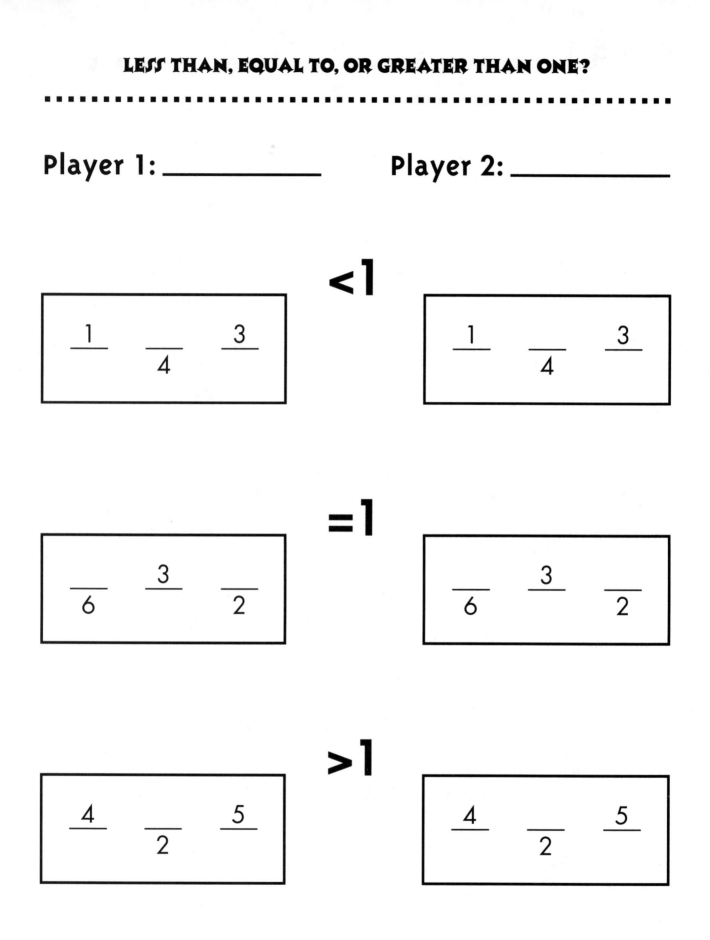

THE 10K CHALLENGE

Skills

Relate common fractions (tenths) to decimals

Name fractions greater than one on a number line

Add and subtract tenths

Ready

Two players

Regular die labeled 1 to 6

Two colored markers or crayons

Two pencils

Game board

Set

Both players are running a 10K race. The shorter player begins. That player records progress on the racecourse in decimal fractions. The other player records progress in common fractions.

Play

Roll the die. The number shows how many **tenths** you gain in the race. Use a color to trace your cumulative distance on one side of the course. Record your progress after each roll by writing a decimal fraction or a common fraction. If you land at a tree, you lose a turn. If you land at a water stand, you can roll again. If you land at a dropped sweatband, you must go back 0.3 km.

The first player to cross the finish line is the winner.

Play Again

Use a centimeter ruler to design another racecourse. Race again in the same way.

THE 10K CHALLENGE

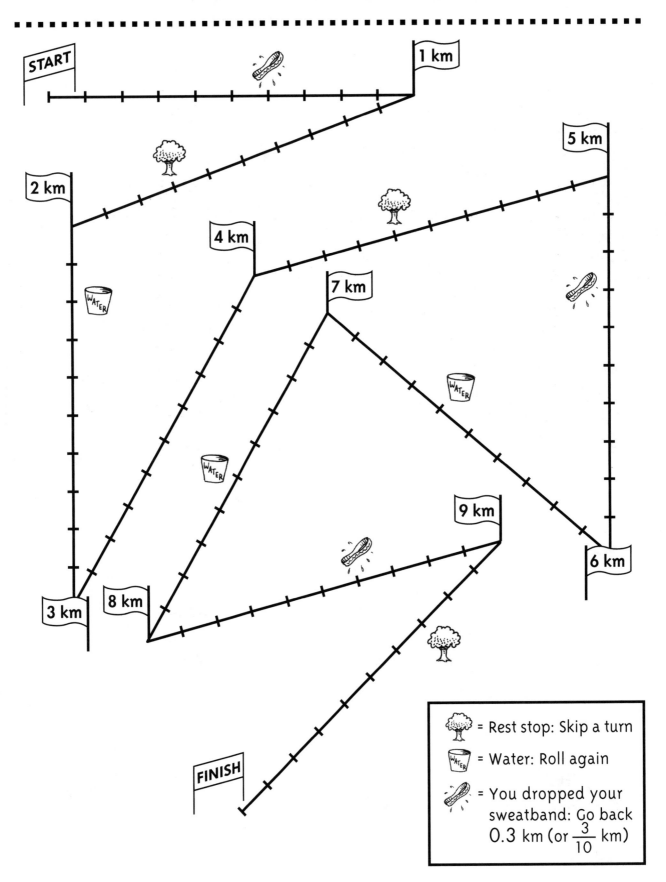

START

1 km

5 km

2 km

4 km

7 km

WATER

WATER

9 km

WATER

3 km

8 km

6 km

FINISH

= Rest stop: Skip a turn

= Water: Roll again

= You dropped your sweatband: Go back 0.3 km (or $\frac{3}{10}$ km)

MEASURING MAGIC BEANS

Skills

Use fractions to measure in inches

Add fractions

Ready

Two players

Make a fraction die labeled $1"$, $\frac{1}{2}"$, $\frac{1}{2}"$, $\frac{1}{4}"$, $\frac{1}{4}"$, $\frac{1}{8}"$

Colored markers or crayons

Game board

Set

The player who has longer feet is Player 1.

Play

Roll the die to see how much your bean plant grows. Start at the bean. Color in the stem to show how long it has grown. Mark the stem and write its total length after each roll. Take turns rolling the die and coloring the stem.

The first player to land exactly on the 8-inch mark is the winner. You cannot go beyond it. If you roll a number you cannot use, your turn ends.

Play Again

Use a fraction die labeled $1"$, $\frac{1}{2}"$, $\frac{1}{4}"$, $\frac{1}{8}"$, $\frac{3}{4}"$, $\frac{5}{8}"$

MEASURING MAGIC BEANS

Jack gave you some of his magic bean seeds. Watch how quickly they grow!

Player 1: _____   Player 2: _____

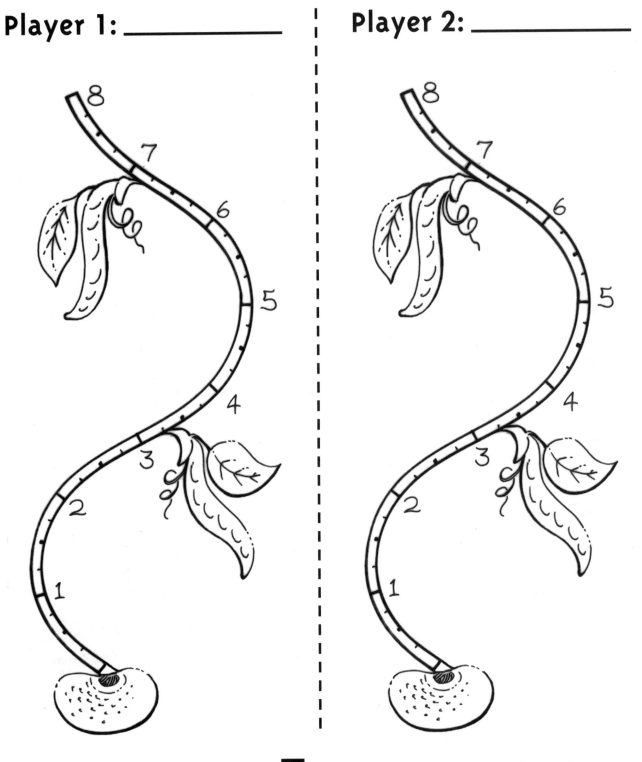

Skills

Use an array to name fractions of a set
Find fractional parts of a number

Ready

Small group
Make a fraction die labeled $\frac{1}{2}$, $\frac{1}{3}$, $\frac{1}{4}$, $\frac{1}{6}$, $\frac{2}{3}$, $\frac{1}{12}$
75–100 doughnuts (use beans, chips, or any type of counter)
Pencils
Paper cups (or use the space marked SOLD on each game board)
One game board for each player

Set

The player who has the longest middle name begins. All players put one counter on each doughnut on the game board. Have a supply of counters within reach of all players.

Play

Roll the die to see what fraction of the doughnuts a customer orders. Take that fraction of doughnuts off your game board and place them in a cup or on the space marked SOLD. Record the sale. Replace the sold doughnuts on your board. For example, you roll $\frac{1}{3}$, take four doughnuts off your board and record $\frac{1}{3}$ of 12 = 4.

Keep playing in the same way until all players have rolled five times. The player who sold the most doughnuts is the winner.

Play Again

Draw 24 doughnuts on a game board. Use a fraction die labeled with six of these fractions: $\frac{1}{2}$, $\frac{1}{3}$, $\frac{2}{3}$, $\frac{3}{4}$, $\frac{5}{6}$, $\frac{3}{8}$, $\frac{7}{8}$, $\frac{5}{12}$, $\frac{11}{12}$.

ONE DOZEN DOUGHNUTS

Always keep 12 doughnuts on your board. Five customers order doughnuts in a most unusual way. They name the fraction that they would like. Roll the die to see what fraction each customer orders.

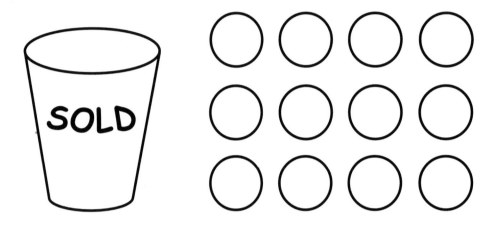

Record how many doughnuts you sell each time.

Roll	How many did you sell?
1	
2	
3	
4	
5	
Total Sold:	

How many doughnuts did you sell altogether? _____
The doughnut shop that sells the most doughnuts is the best in town!

Skill

Recognize equivalent fractions

Ready

Small group

Fraction die labeled $\frac{1}{2}$, $\frac{1}{3}$, $\frac{1}{4}$, $\frac{1}{6}$, $\frac{1}{8}$, $\frac{1}{12}$

10 Counters for each player (use beans, chips, or any type of counter)

One game board for each player

Set

The player who lives nearest the school rolls the die and calls out the fraction rolled for each round of the game.

Play

After each roll of the die, the fraction is called out. All players try to cover an equivalent fraction on their game boards. Try to make a four-square.

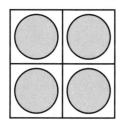

The first player to make a four-square is the winner. The winner rolls the die and calls the fractions for the next game.

Play Again

Be first to make a nine-square to win.

And Again!

For two players. User counters in two colors and one game board. Try to block each other to keep the other player from making a four-square. Play until all the spaces are covered. The player having the most four-squares is the winner.

EQUIVALENT FRACTION FOUR-SQUARE

$\dfrac{2}{4}$	$\dfrac{4}{16}$	$\dfrac{3}{24}$	$\dfrac{2}{6}$	$\dfrac{4}{24}$	$\dfrac{3}{12}$	$\dfrac{4}{8}$
$\dfrac{2}{16}$	$\dfrac{3}{6}$	$\dfrac{5}{20}$	$\dfrac{2}{12}$	$\dfrac{2}{24}$	$\dfrac{4}{12}$	$\dfrac{3}{36}$
$\dfrac{3}{18}$	$\dfrac{4}{12}$	$\dfrac{4}{16}$	$\dfrac{2}{4}$	$\dfrac{3}{36}$	$\dfrac{2}{8}$	$\dfrac{3}{18}$
$\dfrac{2}{24}$	$\dfrac{2}{6}$	$\dfrac{2}{12}$	$\dfrac{3}{24}$	$\dfrac{3}{6}$	$\dfrac{2}{16}$	$\dfrac{5}{20}$
$\dfrac{2}{8}$	$\dfrac{4}{8}$	$\dfrac{4}{16}$	$\dfrac{3}{9}$	$\dfrac{3}{18}$	$\dfrac{3}{12}$	$\dfrac{3}{9}$
$\dfrac{5}{20}$	$\dfrac{3}{24}$	$\dfrac{4}{12}$	$\dfrac{3}{6}$	$\dfrac{4}{24}$	$\dfrac{3}{6}$	$\dfrac{3}{36}$

EQUIVALENT FRACTION TIC-TAC-TOE

Skill

Recognize equivalent fractions

Ready

Two players

Fraction die labeled $\frac{1}{2}$, $\frac{2}{3}$, $\frac{3}{4}$, $\frac{5}{6}$, $\frac{7}{8}$, $\frac{11}{12}$

20 counters, 10 each of two different colors

Game board

Set

The player who has the shorter first name begins. Each player takes counters of one color.

Play

Roll the die and cover an equivalent fraction on the game board with a counter. Take turns and keep playing in the same way.

The first player to cover three fractions in a row in any direction is the winner.

Play Again

To win, you must be first to cover four fractions in a row in any direction.

EQUIVALENT FRACTION TIC-TAC-TOE

$\dfrac{15}{18}$	$\dfrac{4}{8}$	$\dfrac{6}{8}$	$\dfrac{10}{15}$	$\dfrac{6}{12}$
$\dfrac{4}{6}$	$\dfrac{9}{12}$	$\dfrac{22}{24}$	$\dfrac{14}{16}$	$\dfrac{35}{40}$
$\dfrac{12}{16}$	$\dfrac{25}{30}$	$\dfrac{3}{6}$	$\dfrac{44}{48}$	$\dfrac{5}{10}$
$\dfrac{28}{32}$	$\dfrac{2}{4}$	$\dfrac{10}{12}$	$\dfrac{6}{9}$	$\dfrac{18}{24}$
$\dfrac{8}{12}$	$\dfrac{33}{36}$	$\dfrac{15}{20}$	$\dfrac{20}{24}$	$\dfrac{21}{24}$

Skill

Add fractions having like denominators

Ready

Small group

Two fraction dice labeled $\frac{1}{6}$, $\frac{2}{6}$, $\frac{3}{6}$, $\frac{4}{6}$, $\frac{5}{6}$, $\frac{6}{6}$

Colored markers or crayons

Game board for each player

Set

The player whose birthday is closest to January 1 begins. Write all the sums listed below in the triangles on your game board. Write each fraction three or four times to fill all the triangles.

$\frac{2}{6}$, $\frac{3}{6}$, $\frac{4}{6}$, $\frac{5}{6}$, $\frac{6}{6}$, $\frac{7}{6}$, $\frac{8}{6}$, $\frac{9}{6}$, $\frac{10}{6}$, $\frac{11}{6}$, $\frac{12}{6}$

Play

Take turns rolling the dice. Add the fractions you roll and color a triangle space that shows the sum.

The first player to make a path of touching triangles from the bottom to the summit of the mountain is the winner. The triangles in the path must touch sides.

Play Again

Write these sums in the triangles on your game board and play again in the same way.

$\frac{1}{3}$, $\frac{1}{2}$, $\frac{2}{3}$, $\frac{5}{6}$, 1, $1\frac{1}{6}$, $1\frac{1}{3}$, $1\frac{1}{2}$, $1\frac{2}{3}$, $1\frac{5}{6}$, 2

SUM IT SUMMIT

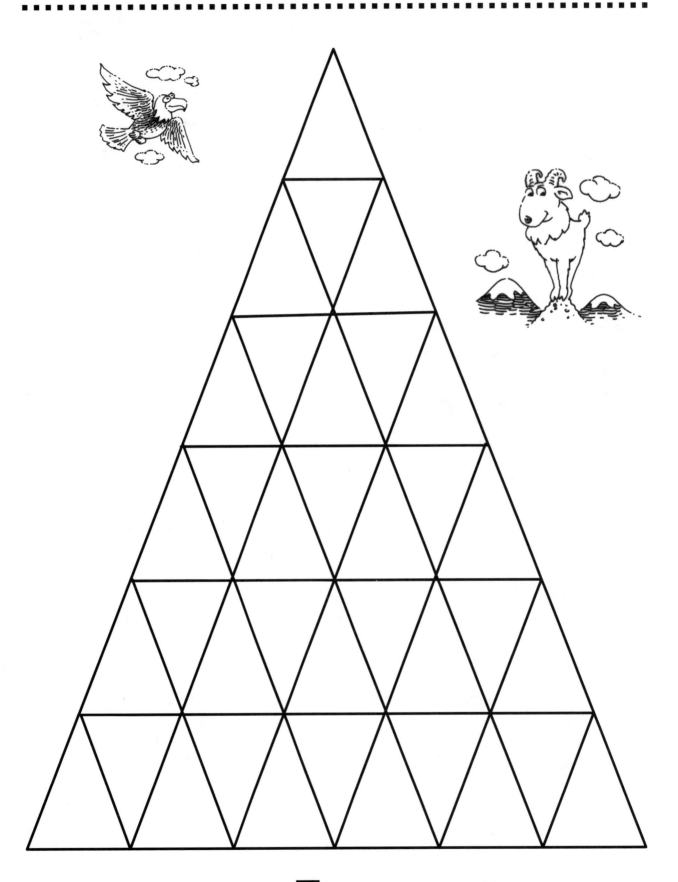

HIGH OR LOW?

Skills

Add fractions having like and unlike denominators
Compare fractions less than, equal to, and greater than one

Ready

Small group
Make a die labeled 1, 2, 2, 3, 4, 12
Pencils
One game board for each player
Cut along the dotted line to make two boards

Set

The player who has the shortest hair begins and gets to roll the die and call out the numbers for the first game.

Play

The first player chooses to play a round of Highest Sum (H) or Lowest Sum (L). All players circle H (for highest sum) or L (for lowest sum) . After each roll of the die, all players write the number rolled as a numerator or a denominator in one of the four boxes. Once you write a number, it cannot be changed. Keep playing for three more rolls until all four boxes are filled in to make an addition sentence.

Find the sum of your addition sentence. The player having the winning sum (highest or lowest) is the winner for that game. That player gets to roll the die, call the numbers, and choose to play a round of highest or lowest sum for the next game.

The player who wins the most games is the grand winner.

Play Again

Use a die labeled with six of these numbers: 2, 3, 4, 5, 6, 8, 10, 12.

HIGH OR LOW?

Name: _____   **Name:** _____

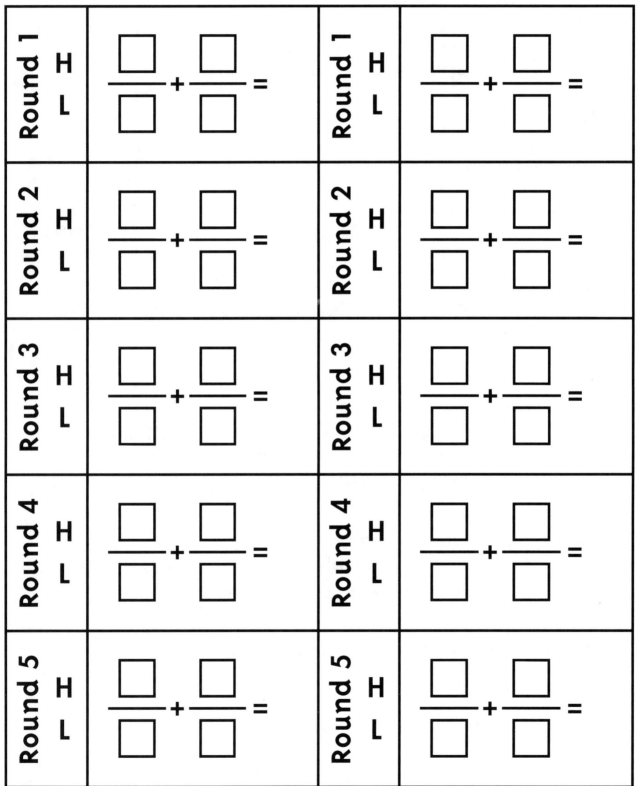

SUM-DIFFERENCE

Skills

Add and subtract fractions having like and unlike denominators

Compare fractions

Ready

Small group

Two fraction dice labeled $\frac{1}{2}$, $\frac{1}{3}$, $\frac{1}{4}$, $\frac{1}{6}$, $\frac{1}{8}$, $\frac{1}{12}$ and $\frac{1}{2}$, $\frac{2}{3}$, $\frac{3}{4}$, $\frac{5}{6}$, $\frac{7}{8}$, $\frac{11}{12}$

Pencils

One game board for each player

Set

The player who sits closest to the door begins. Play proceeds in a clockwise direction.

Play

Take turns. Roll both dice. Write the two fractions you roll on your game board. Find their sum, then find their difference.

	Sum	Difference
	$\frac{1}{4} + \frac{5}{6} =$	$\frac{5}{6} - \frac{1}{4} =$
	$\frac{3}{12} + \frac{10}{12} = \frac{13}{12}$ or $1\frac{1}{12}$	$\frac{10}{12} - \frac{3}{12} = \frac{7}{12}$

After each round, compare your sums and differences with the other player. After each round, find which player has the largest sum and circle it. Then find which player has the smallest difference and circle it.

There can be two winners—the player having the most sums circled and the player having the most differences circled.

Play Again

Use two dice labeled $\frac{1}{2}$, $\frac{2}{3}$, $\frac{3}{4}$, $\frac{5}{6}$, $\frac{7}{8}$, $\frac{11}{12}$ and play in the same way.

SUM-DIFFERENCE

Roll 2 fraction dice. Write a number sentence to show the sum. Then write a number sentence to show the difference. Compare your answers with other players. After each round, circle the **largest sum** and the **smallest difference**.

	Sum	Difference
Round 1		
Round 2		
Round 3		
Round 4		
Round 5		

How many **sums** did you circle? _____

How many **differences** did you circle? _____